THE CAELi Review

VOLUME 1 No. 1 | November 2023

LETTER FROM THE EDITOR

SJ ANDERSON
When Random Rules: The Power of Textual
Sortilege to Enhance Astrological Signification   PAGE 5

HILLARY SCHOFIELD
Ratio   PAGE 8

BARIS ILHAN
From Nasir al-Din Tusi to Copernicus   PAGE 9

GIACOMO ALBANO
Ancient Egypt and the Stars: Archaeoastronomical
Evidence of a Secret Sacred Astronomy   PAGE 13

THEA N. ANDERSON
The Imperial 95: An Astrological Excavation
of Convict Leasing in Sugar Land, Texas   PAGE 23

DREW LEVANTI
Satellite   PAGE 38

ANNE C. SCHNEIDER
Relocating the Solar Return Chart:
A Report from Practical Experience   PAGE 40

GRAY CRAWFORD
Pole Star Epochs:
From the Dragon to the Bear   PAGE 49

revelore press

CONTRIBUTORS TO THIS ISSUE:

Anne C. Schneider has been studying traditional astrology for over 30 years and advises clients, serves the astrological community, and organizes and lectures at conferences across Europe. She publishes regularly in the German journal *MERIDIAN*, and is co-author of the anthology *Karma und Astrologie*. sagitta@gmx.de

Baris Ilhan, CA, NCGR, a leading astrologer in Turkey since 1993, owns a publishing house and an astrology school: The Ilhan Astrology Institute. She teaches, writes, and lectures regularly, and researches Ottoman and Islamic astrology. Member of NCGR, ISAR, AFA, AFAN, AA, OPA and Advisory Board of NCGR, president of NCGR Turkey chapter. Her two books are: *The Puberty Age of Adults: Planetary Cycles* and the textbook *Astrology Lessons*. www.barisilhan.com

Guided by traditional technique and intuitive insight, **Drew Levanti** is an Orphic astrologer, using poetics, prayer and ceremonial interventions to help clients untangle the webs of fate and remember who they really are.

Giacomo Albano is a specialist in stellar astrology, horary and electional astrology and astrological magic based in Italy. Among his latest publications are: *Advanced Stellar Astrology*, *Mundane Stellar Astrology*, *Ancient Egypt, Jerusalem and the Stars*.... www.astrologiaprevisionale.net

Gray Crawford is a natal, horary, and electional astrologer and teacher from Olympia, WA. Gray brings a relational approach to astrology drawing on techniques from ancient and modern sources, including Hellenistic, magical, mythic-archetypal, and psychological astrology. graycrawford.net .

Hillary Schofield is an astrologer, a writer, a forager, gardener, and home herbalist. Her chapbook *WREST* appeared through Revelore Press in 2019.

SJ Anderson, astrologer and writer influenced by studies in Hellenistic astrology, Theravada Buddhism, and Sivananda yoga, and lifetime member of the International Society for Astrological Research (ISAR). His writing has been featured in publications such as Ignota Press, *Wellbeing Astrology Guide*, *India Times*, *Daily Express*, *Mashable*, and more. www.sjanderson144.com

Thea Anderson is an astrologer and writer whose work has been featured in *Infinite Constellations*, the *Triangle House Review*, and *The Mountain Astrologer*. She is Chief of Staff at CHANI, Inc. She was raised in Sugar Land and Missouri City, Texas. Her ancestors were enslaved in Texas and family members have been incarcerated in this country.

LETTER FROM THE EDITOR

Dear Esteemed Readers,

WELCOME TO THE INAUGURAL ISSUE OF *The CAELi Review*, a quarterly publication of celestial arts stemming from the CAELi Institute. I am honored to pen this first letter as its editor. This journal offers a platform to explore the cosmic *"tilt"* of life, a theme that pervades the pages you hold here.

Life often presents us with challenges, making us feel as though the world tilts against us despite our best intentions. However, our celestial studies remind us that these challenges are but steps in the grand design of the cosmic machinery. Without this slant, life would lack its necessary complexity.

Imagine a world...where the planets always moved forward, the zodiac signs rose perfectly straight, the year had a fixed 360 days, and the Earth's axis had no tilt, resulting in unchanging seasons. Such a world would leave us with little to learn and explore. Instead, we should view these "slanting" signs as messages from the creator, encouraging us to embrace life's variations and find the beauty in its unpredictability.

The articles in this inaugural issue of *The CAELi Review* reflect this cosmic angle, both in the realms of society and science. From the injustices in the American Deep South to personal journeys of overcoming our inner inclinations through astrological pilgrimages and the often-overlooked Islamic scientific achievements overshadowed by those of the later European Renaissance. We are also thrilled to present two articles delving into the Earth's axial tilt and precessional cycle, unveiling captivating mysteries about the grand astrological cycles of time. As this first issue of the journal came together, I met up with Petr Soural in Prague. He's the designer of Astro-Seek.com, and he agreed to let us work with his software to make charts for the journal. Thank you, Petr!

If you look closely at our cover, you will notice that our design mirrors the inclinations of our craft. Our name juts forth at a 23.5-degree angle, the same angle that our Earth's axis tilts toward the radiant Sun. This interval symbolizes the space between perfection and imperfection, allowing room for our creative expressions. In the realm of astrology, it is the diversity and contradictions that nourish our interpretations, discussions, and artistic endeavors. The disagreements, varied perspectives, and profound questions enrich our comprehension of the cosmos and the human experience.

We are fortunate to be practitioners of this Mercurial art as we celebrate the space between the lines, nurturing the art within the science of observing celestial signs. Without this margin, we would have only facts, devoid of the room for personal catharsis that transforms our emotions and feelings into creative expressions. This is the essence of our journal's tagline, "Celestial Arts Quarterly." Every three months, in tune with the cross-quarters of the tropical seasons, we present fresh ideas, voices, and perspectives, aligning us with the "in-between" moments of our time and space.

Our mission is to showcase talented astrologers from diverse backgrounds and practices, fostering conversations about the developments in our astrological zeitgeist. We aim to explore cutting-edge approaches to working with, recognizing, and living within the astrological tradition. The grand tapestry of the cosmos unfolds before us, weaving together a rich array of insights and philosophies, and we hope you relish the journey.

>   Continue to create within the cosmic "tilt,"
>   Cameron Cassidy
>   Editor, *The CAELi Review*
>   Heidelberg, Germany
>   November 7, 2023

SJ ANDERSON

When Random Rules: The Power of Textual Sortilege to Enhance Astrological Signification

ASTROLOGY IS A PRACTICE DEEPLY INTERTWINED with textual representations. One sub-definition of astrology might go as far as being, "astrology is the production of text expressing how observed celestial phenomena are meaningful." Astrologers measure the heavens and discover patterns correlating to those measurements. They then memorialize that knowledge into written works. Many such language forms live on well beyond the time frame of their creation. Astrologers center these written explications and many produce their own. Engaging astrological texts becomes a continuous dynamic within the discipline.

Much of contemporary astrology is inextricably linked with the written word. Meme culture superimposes astrological significance over pop culture imagery by adding zodiacal or planetary vocabulary. Thousands of succinct delineations are written hourly and presented in an unceasing stream across internet platforms. The persistent centrality of the written word within astrological discourse is as apparent as it's ever been. Immersion in an overabundance of books is a right of passage for astrology students, one that very often soon follows the initial fervor for the subject.

Astrological texts extend beyond mere printed descriptions. They are access points, they are pathways into the living worlds of the planets and other associated astrological symbols. Astrologers interface with these symbols via the texts that expound upon them. The written word in this context possesses animacy. An ancient manuscript, a social media post, a magazine page, all are vital conduits through which humans connect with the ensouled sky. Published language becomes the vital pulse, the crucial medium of an archetype's articulation.

The sheer variety of astrological texts makes them ripe for recombination. Remixing the words and phrases of planetary symbology distills layers of meaning. New, never before expressed, textual frontiers emerge. Hitherto unknown phraseologies generate novel significations. The vast landscape of the astrological lexicon contains a near infinity of permutations. And so like language itself, astrological meanings are fluid. Textual amalgamation and re-amalgamation functions to vivify and widen extant astrologies.

Adopting sortilege based divination techniques—for example, using a random number generator to select and combine lines of text in a William S. Burroughs cut-up style[1]—produces unexpected and profound meanings. Two textual artifacts derived from the same foundational concept—a planetary archetype, for example—can be intermixed. Consider that a small excised fragment of text contains some essence of the whole. When parts of diverse texts about similar topics are merged—no matter their languages of origin or the timelines of their generation—the underlying archetype is expanded through a kind of linguistic arithmetic. Like neurons seeking new networks of connectivity, these interplays-of-text breathe fresh life into understandings of astrological symbols, and particularly when sculpted by the minds of living astrologers.

This is text as a dynamic entity: waiting to be unlocked, asking to be molded, demanding to be reorganized. Consider the third line from Valens' paragraph delineating Venus, taken from the widely circulated PDF of Riley's translation. Chosen using a random number generator, this line says that Venus signifies "companionship, the acquisition of property, the purchase of ornaments, agreements on favorable terms."[2] The snippet provides a shard of one ancient view of Venus, one anchored in a more physicalist paradigm. However, when we juxtapose this with the fifteenth paragraph from Dane Rudhyar's *New Mansions for New Men*—also chosen at random—an entirely new dimension emerges. Rudyhar writes on Venus:

> Ours is the task, humans born of this Earth, to produce as flowers the nectar that shall draw to us the "celestial Bees." This is our transmutation and our alchemy. From the roots of our earthly nature, deep in the pelvic regions, through the stem of our spine, the mystic sap of conscious life must rise, until it becomes within the hollow of the brain —the Ajna center of the Hindus—the spiritual nectar of a life well lived in terms of creative significance, of harmony that is love, and of beauty.[3]

Reading Valens against Rudhyar enriches notions of Venus. Their combination suggests that the joys of companionship and the beauty of ornaments are linked with creativity's spiritual essence. The intersection where seen and unseen realms overlap becomes a key to unlocking Venusian potency. The two texts together point to a generativity purified by spirit, a force that undergirds outer adornment and social cohesion, that lubricates human relational connectivity.

We can extend this merger further into new textual forms articulating Venus: "the nectar that draws in companionship," or "acquisition for the purpose of harmonizing with beauty," or "adornment imbued with the mystic sap of conscious life." Astrological texts, then, are not static repositories of knowledge. They are at their root dynamic. Words and phrases can be mixed to derive fresh meaning, to offer previously unknown outlets through which astrology's living symbols can maneuver and thereby flourish.

Notes

1. Robin Lydenberg, "Cut-up: Negative Poetics in William S. Burroughs and Roland Barthes," *Comparative Literature Studies* 15, no. 4 (December 1978): 414-430, https://www.jstor.org/stable/40245850. Lydenberg delves into the disruptive and innovative nature of the "cut-up" technique pioneered by William S. Burroughs, which involves cutting up text into single words or phrases and then randomly rearranging them to create new text. She notes, "Both Barthes and Burroughs are engaged in a terroristic enterprise, a violent challenge to traditional expectations and assumptions. The cut-up texts they produce attempt to counteract the parasitism and the numbing lubricity of conventional language with open structures of meaning which permit reversibility, expansion, anonymity and ultimately silence."
2. Vettius Valens, *The Anthology*, trans. Mark T. Riley, online, December 2010, accessed October 1, 2023, http://www.csus.edu/indiv/r/rileymt/Vettius%20Valens%20entire.pdf.
3. Dane Rudhyar, *New Mansions for New Men: A Spiritual Interpretation of Astrology in the Light of Universal Symbolism* (1938), accessed October 1, 2023, https://khaldea.com/rudhyar/nmnm/nmnm _ venus.php.

HILLARY SCHOFIELD

ratio

to be slow
is to be
close

... a poem from *WREST* (Revelore, 2019).

BARIS ILHAN

From Nasir al-Din Tusi to Copernicus

NASIR AL-DIN TUSI (1201–74) IS NOT WELL KNOWN in the Western world. I encountered him through my research for *The Astrology of the Ottoman Empire*, wherein I tried to establish whether the famous astronomer and mathematician Ali Qushji—who was influential in the madrasa at Constantinople during the reign of Mehmed the Conqueror—was also an astrologer. While attending the Ali Qushji symposium at Istanbul University, I was taken by Prof. F. Jamil Ragep's talk on Copernicus' role in adapting and transferring Islamic astronomical knowledge to the West. At the time, I had also been researching whether astrology was taught in Ottoman madrasas, wondering about which source texts scholars might have used. Through further research, I came across Tusi's book on calendar preparation and astrology that led me to his other astrological works. I worked with the professors from Istanbul University who had translated Tusi's manuscripts, and presented the findings to the Western world for the first time at UAC in Denver, Colorado. The presentation resonated. Other than its contribution to the history of non-western astrology, there were two reasons for the talk's reception. First, in the Western World, scientific studies in the East are only thought to have occurred during the 11th and 12th centuries. However, Tusi's works were written in the 13th century, at least a hundred years later. Second, in the early 1900s, Western historians of science had begun investigating Islamic influence on Copernicus' works. Owing to research like Prof. Recep's, it has become clear that Islamic scholars like Tusi had provided much of the foreground for Copernicus' inventions. This article expands on my initial presentation of these ideas at UAC.

Construction of the Observatory

Nasreddin al-Tusi was born at Tus, Khorasan in 1201, and died at Baghdad in 1274. He completed his education in philosophy, medicine, astronomy/astrology and mathematics at Nishapur. During his studies, he examined Ibn Sina's philosophical works before authoring a commentary on them. His contribution ensured the revival of mathematics, astronomy, and Ibn Sina's philosophy in Islamic discourses. In his late 20s, Tusi joined the Ismailis—either by force or voluntarily—and started living at Alamut Castle. In those years, he wrote important works using Alamut's rich library and was active in its intellectual life. He remained there until the Mongol siege of the castle in 1256, and later became Hulagu Khan's advisor and astrologer. In this role, he advised the construction of an observatory in Meraga in 1259. Science historian Ord. Prof. Dr. Aydin Sayili accepts this period as the peak of Islamic observatories.

According to Sayili, after hearing about the high costs of establishing the observatory, Hulagu Khan questioned its necessity. Tusi replied:

> Let's say you told someone to throw a big rock from a high point. This will make a very loud sound and will scare anyone who doesn't know that something big is falling from above. Only you and the man you command will remain calm because you know that the rock will fall.[1]

This story demonstrates that the purpose of the observatory was astrological. However, Tusi probably had another motivation: he wanted to criticize and correct Ptolemy's astronomy.

The criticism and reformulation attempt of the ancient Greek tradition in astronomy by Islamic scientists began long before the Meraga observatory and reached its peak in the 14th century. Indeed, some of its foremost astronomers had started their reform efforts long before its establishment: they were probably invited to the observatory because of their involvement. In addition to Tusi, the leading scholars at the observatory were al-Shirazi, al-Urdi and al-Magribi.

In his astronomical masterpiece *al-Tadhkira fi'ilm al-hay'a* written at Meraga 1261, Tusi presented a new model of planetary motion, very different from that of Ptolemy. Through his model, he proved that cyclic motion could turn into linear motion. Today, Tusi's model is known as the Tusi Couple.

Copernicus' Need

In the second half of the 20th century, historians of science determined that the mathematical structure of Copernican astronomy could not have been established with the information in classical Greek works alone. To develop his theory, Copernicus must have

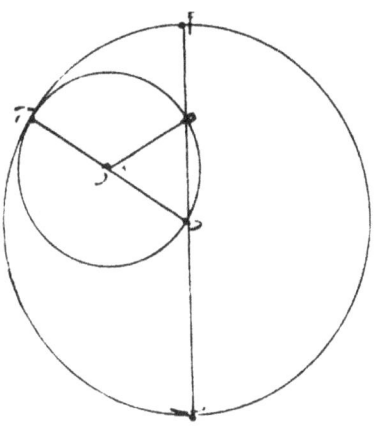 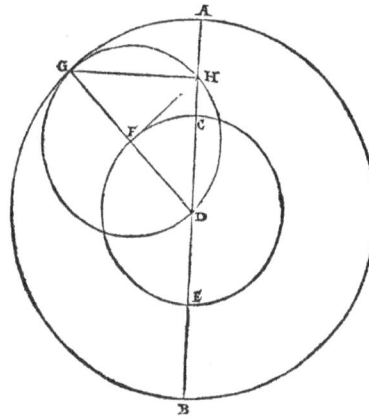

Figure 1: On the left is the Tūsī couple in Naṣīr al-Dīn's *Tadhkira fī 'ilm al-hay'a*. On the right is the same found in the Edito Princeps of *De revolutionibus* (Nuremberg, 1543), fol. 67a.[2]

relied on two mathematical theorems that classical Greeks had not accounted for. The two theorems in question were the Tusi Couple and Urdi Lemma, first put forward by Tusi and al-Urdi, respectively, during their time at the Meraga observatory.

One of the greatest points of evidence supporting the claim that Copernicus drew on Islamic texts is Tusi's (13th century) and Copernicus' (15th century) use of the same letters to mark significant points (Fig. 1). The second interesting point is that although Copernicus used these theorems, he did not present proof of their origin. This shows that he must have taken the theorems from somewhere else, having not developed them himself. Copernicus' appropriation of the theorems is made even clearer in a letter Kepler wrote to his teacher in the 17th century. In it, Kepler asked why Copernicus had not provided justification for the theorems. It's puzzling that Copernicus used the Tusi Couple and Urdi Lemma without mentioning Tusi and al-Urdi. One likely reason is that there was a generally negative attitude towards Islam at that time, as the Ottoman Empire was knocking on Europe's door. It might not have been appropriate for Copernicus to credit Islamic scholars under these conditions.

How Tusi and al-Urdi's works—which had not been translated into Latin at the time—came into Copernicus's hands is a separate research topic. According to one theory, these works first went to

Trabizon, then to Constantinople, and from there to Italy where a Latin copy of Tusi's work was found in the 16th century.

The findings here are significant. They indicate that the scientists of the Meraga observatory not only did original work in mathematics and astronomy, but also built the foundations for Copernicus' later theories. So much so that if they had changed the places of the Earth and the Sun in their writings, they might have been the initiators of the Copernican revolution. In some circles, their achievements are referred to as the Meraga School Revolution. We might call theirs the Scientific Renaissance before the Renaissance.

Notes

This article was first published in the newspaper *Radikal* 2, 29/06/2008.
1. Aydin Sayili, *The Observatory in Islam and Its Place in the General History of the Observatory*, Turkish Historical Society, 1960.
2. https://doi.org/10.1177/002182861404500203

GIACOMO ALBANO

Ancient Egypt and the Stars: Archaeoastronomical Evidence of a Secret Sacred Astronomy

WHEN ANCIENT EGYPTIANS WANTED to emphasize solar or lunar phenomena, they oriented their monuments to solstices and lunistices. In *Ancient Egypt, Jerusalem and the Stars: Archaeoastronomical Evidence of a Secret Sacred Astronomy*, I examine major ancient Egyptian monuments, to demonstrate that Egyptians oriented their buildings to *stellar* phenomena, too. My findings indicate that the real (and secret) objective of Egyptian architects was to capture the rising or setting points of Sirius, the stars of Orion, and those of the Big Dipper at their minimum or maximum declinations along the horizon. As it so happens, these stars hold fundamental importance in Egyptian theology , which we will see proven to be aligned with their temples in astonishing astronomical precision.

Following the apparent position of the stars in the sky at the time of the monuments' construction, no temple nor pyramid seems aligned with the stars of Orion. Among the pyramids, none are apparently oriented to Sirius. But it's unlikely that Egyptian theology's most significant stars were completely ignored in the orientations of its sacred buildings. It was precisely the deceased pharaoh who was assimilated to Osiris, whose astral manifestation was Orion. This symbolic fusion between Osiris and Orion connected the deity physically to the temples, and also the priests working the rituals within them.

The relationship between Egyptian monuments and stars becomes clear when we go back to the years when Orion and Sirius were at their extreme declinations: their stopping points along the horizon. A star's stopping point refers to locations north or south along the local horizon where it rises at its minimum declination (lowest stopping point to the North of the Horizon) or its maximum declination (upper stopping point to the South of the Horizon). Using these critical positions of the relevant stars, Egyptian temples and pyramids clearly point to their rising, setting, and culmination points.

The reasons why Egyptians oriented their temples this way are esoteric. However, it's clear that Egyptian initiates believed that stars had extraordinary powers in these extreme phases of their cycles, which happen just twice on either end of the 26,000 year precessional cycle. Belief in the efficacy of these powers is easily verifiable in the normal practice of mundane astrology, where stars at their minimum or maximum declinations represent the main causes of epochal events throughout history. They are also easy to spot because they are the stars that culminate at midnight during the solstice periods, which due to precession, notably changes stars every few hundred years.

The main problem that arises in Egyptian archaeoastronomy is the timeline of events. Since the stars that were significant for the Egyptians had reached their extreme declinations many thousands of years before they began building their monuments, it's unclear how they knew which points on the horizon to align their buildings with. Perhaps the answer lies in the astronomical alignments of the oldest megalithic site found to date: Nabta Playa.

Nestled in the middle of the Sahara desert, Nabta Playa is the remains of an ancient ceremonial site that predates Egyptian civilization by many thousands of years. Its precise origins are lost to the sands of time. However, it provides clues about how ancient peoples used stone landmarks to track the positions of stars for tens of thousands of years.

If the hypothesis of archeoastronomy holds, it is because ancient people not only attributed importance to more simply observable phenomena like the equinoxes and the solstices, but to the precessional motion of the stars as well. In this system, the solstices and the equinoxes are important because they represent privileged moments in important stellar cycles. In fact, the alignments found at Nabta Playa demonstrate that some orientations that seem to be just solstitial, were more likely used to observe the change in the precessional position of the stars at particular times of the year.

Importantly, a star remains linked to its two points of maximum and minimum declination for its entire precessional cycle, even when the declination points make the star rise or set somewhere in the range between a star's two extremes, which happens most of the time when a star isn't at its precessed maximum or minimum declination. In other words, the points on the horizon where a star rises and sets in its two extreme declination phases still remain linked to the star for 26,000 years. The alignments found at Nabta Playa are significant, because they would have pointed later Egyptian people to these unwavering declination points of their most sacred stars.

Let's examine some examples of how this technique was applied to Egyptian monuments. The interested reader will find much more material in *Ancient Egypt, Jerusalem and the Stars*..., but to start, these techniques rely on knowledge of the last minimum and maximum declination points reached by the stars. For this purpose, I published the ebook *The Journey of the Stars*. Tables of minimum and maximum star declinations in the current precessional cycle in which I provide a list of the minimum and maximum declinations of all stars.

The head of Osiris and the mystery of Abydos

Abydos, considered a sacred place since ancient times, is still shrouded in an aura of mystery. It is home to one of the oldest necropolises for early-dynasty kings, and an important epicenter of the Cult of Osiris, whose head was supposed to be buried there. Important enough to note here, Orion was envisioned by the Egyptians to be Osiris' astral correlate. Let's examine how the stars of Orion are precisely aligned to the major axes of this temple, when rising at the maximum and minimum declinations.

Shunet El Zebib was constructed in Abydos around 2750 BCE by the ancient Egyptian king Khasekhemwy—the last ruler of the Second

Figure 1: South-eastern wall of the Shunet El Zebib (شونة الزبيب)[1]

Dynasty. The Shunet was built as a kind of burial enclosure where the deceased king was entombed and worshiped.

The structure is a prime example of perfect (or almost perfect) intercardinal orientation, and typical of monuments constructed in this early period of Egyptian history. The intercardinal points are the average points between the four cardinal points, namely 45° (the midpoint between 0° North and 90° East), 135° (between 90° East and 180° South), 225° (between 180° South and 270° West) and 315° (between 270° West and 0° North).

The azimuth of the Shunet Temple's main axis is about 136°, in between the Eastern and Southern directions. This is exactly the rising azimuth of the stars of Orion's head (phi1, phi2, and Meissa [lambda Orionis]) at their minimum declination. More generally, the structure's main axis also points to the rising azimuth of the upper part of Orion, which includes Bellatrix and Betelgeuse, his left and right shoulders, at their lowest declinations. It also coincides with the heliacal rising of Bellatrix from around 10,500 BCE. The direction of Shunet's other major axis is 226° southwest (with its reciprocal azimuth at 46° northeast—both almost right on the sacred intercardinal directions). At its lowest declination, the main star of Orion's head (Meissa [lambda]) set with an azimuth between 225° and 226°. Orion's phi2 would have also just set at 226°.

Shunet's orientation towards the minimum declination of Orion's head is very significant when we consider that the head of the Egyptian god Osiris was thought to have been buried there.

Lastly, one of the structure's two diagonal axes is oriented to 161°, which aligns precisely with the heliacal rising of Rigel at its minimum declination. Rigel is yet another bright star in Orion, sacred to Osiris, and is located at the bottom of the constellation.

The Ramesseum

In Thebes, Upper Egypt, near the Nile, and only a short distance from the modern city of Luxor, lies the Ramesseum—the funerary temple of Ramesses II. Its construction began around 1277 BCE. It was colloquially known as "the million-year-old house of Ramesses II." Two stone pylons flank the entrance and lead to the temple courtyard. The first courtyard contains a huge statue of Ramesses, and its remains can still be admired today. In the center of the complex, there was a hypostyle room supported by 48 columns surrounding the inner sanctuary.

Figure 2: Ramesseum Temple²

The complex's famous astronomical room located in the heart of the Ramesseum is clear confirmation that the attending priests practiced astronomy. However, scholars have failed to explain the significance of the Ramasseum's orientation, as that of other Ramesside-era temples like it. The only exception is a number of temples that are clearly oriented to the winter solstice sunrise.

The Ramesseum's major axis has an azimuth of about 135–36° southeast. Another smaller axis is at about 45° exactly on the intercardinal northeast (with 225° being the reciprocal azimuth in the southwest). This is the classic intercardinal direction evidently used in Egypt since the first burials at Abydos. As we've established, the stars of Orion rose and set in this intercardinal direction at their minimum declinations. This is the likely explanation for the recurrence of this temple alignment through Egyptian history. The use of intercardinal directions means that Egyptian architects would not have been trying to point their structures strictly at stars that were visible in the sky. The stars would have significantly changed their rising and setting points by the time of their construction. However, the 135° angle of the Ramasseum's major axis directly corresponds to the rising of Orion's head at their minimum declinations at about 10,700 BCE, while the 45° axis of the temple's minor axis corresponds to their reciprocal setting azimuth. These angles would have remained consistent through the beginning of the complex's construction.

At the time of construction bright stars such as Vega, Arcturus (and Garuxat the reciprocal azimuth) would have also touched the

Ancient Egypt and the ſtars   17

horizon at the intercardinal directions. But those stars are not specifically linked to Egyptian theology, and their association with this axis is not consistent throughout the course of Egyptian history. It's likely that their alignment to the intercardinal directions was seen as a sort of activation point for the stars of Orion at their minimum declinations which were the real objects of temple orientations since the time of Abydos.

But there's more. Thanks to the length of the two sides of the Ramasseum's rectangular building, it happens that its two diagonal axes point towards two other important directions. In this case the target is Sirius: one of the two diagonals points towards its rise at its minimum declination (about 170°, almost due South), the other towards its rise at its maximum (about 103°, almost due East). Orion was identified with Osiris and Sirius with Isis. Given this temple's alignment with exactly the brightest stars of both Orion and Sirius, it's extremely unlikely that this alignment happened by pure chance.

Other royal temples in the western part of Thebes have similar orientations to the intercardinal directions. There is slim reason to doubt that there was a specific intentionality in this choice. For example, the temple of Ramesses III at Medinet Habu points to the same direction, with the diagonal axes of various parts of the building also being oriented to Sirius at its extreme declination. In these cases, the buildings and their axial relationships with the stars enshrine *the fundamental myth* of ancient Egypt—that of Isis and Osiris—in stone. The temples themselves are a symbolic reference to both death (Orion/Osiris) and resurrection (Sirius/Isis, who reassembles the body of Osiris). In the myth that surrounds them, Isis and Osiris give birth to the triumphant Horus, who Ramesses II was associated with. Thus, the symbolic coupling between Isis and Osiris (represented by the axes and diagonals of the Ramesseum), symbolically generate Horus, the divine son destined to defeat Seth before triumphing over the world of the dead and the living. Horus represents the cosmic order that prevails over chaos and transforms the dead pharaohs into imperishable stars or deities.

Egyptian monuments could just as faithfully be called "stone stars" because of their ability to translate complex stellar symbolism—often involving more than one star at the same time—into architectural forms.

Twice each year the sun shines directly into the inner sanctuary, illuminating three of the four figures inside.[3]

Abu Simbel

The Egyptian use of precessional star cycles also explains the famous light phenomenon that occurs each year in Abu Simbel on February 21 and October 21.

Each year on these days, the Sun illuminates statues of the pharaoh, the sun god Amon-Ra and Ra-Horakhty that are placed at the bottom of the sanctuary. Significantly, these are the dates when the Sun's declination paralleled Sirius' maximum declination as it would have been many millennia before. The likely reason the temple at Abu Simbel was positioned this way was so that the Sun could "activate" Sirius (the "occult" Sun) at its extreme declination. It's compelling, considering that these dates don't have another astronomical significance that would justify this choice.

Luxor Temple

Luxor Temple is a large temple complex located on the east bank of the Nile near ancient Thebes. It was dedicated to Amun. During the New Kingdom it was the center of the annual feast of Opet, during

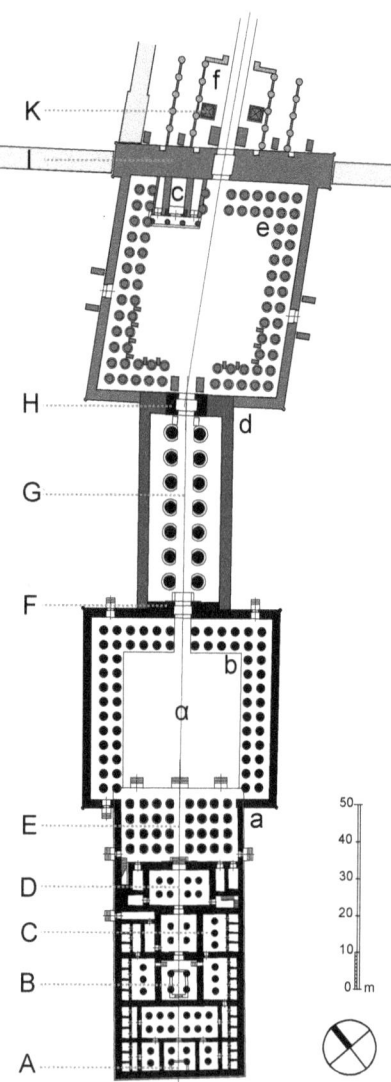

Plan of the Luxor Temple[4]
A) sanctuary of Amun B) sanctuary of the boat C) room of the birth
D) Roman sanctuary E) hypostyle room F) III pylon G) ceremonial
colonnade H) II pylon I) I pylon K) obelisks.
a) temple of Amun (Amenhotep III) b) court of the Sun (Amenhotep
III) c) place of the boat (Thutmose III and Hatshepsut) and sanctuary of
the Theban triad (Ramses II)

which a statue of the god was brought to Luxor along the Nile from the nearby Great Temple of Amun. The construction of Luxor Temple began during the reign of Amenhotep III in the 14th century BCE. The Sanctuary of Amun is located in the deepest part of the temple and was the place where the statue of the god was kept. The sanctuary was the final destination of the Sacred Boat that came from the Great Temple of Amun, whereupon the divinity was thought to be regenerated.

The different orientations of the buildings that form the complex can be explained by the minimum declination points of Orion. Specifically, if we start from the entrance of the temple and proceed gradually towards the innermost parts, we notice an incredible correspondence between the orientations of the buildings and the various parts of the constellation-body of Orion in its minimum declinations, starting from the head and ending at the Belt.

    225° (real setting point of Orion's head)
    222–23° (Bellatrix's real setting)
    219°–20° (Bellatrix's heliacal setting)
    214° (real setting of the Orion's Belt)
    210–11° (heliacal setting of the Orion's Belt and the Sanctuary of Amun)

These phenomena in their time occurred behind the site of the future temple. Following the Luxor Temple's construction, people entering or coming from the North, would be looking at a kind of projection of the astral image of Orion setting at its minimum declination. And, as we know, the stars at their stopping points are always *virtually* present at the same points on the horizon throughout their 26,000-year cycle. In other words, these points on the horizon would have remained impressed by Orion's stars throughout their precessional cycle, retaining their influence even as the visible rising and setting points of its stars would change over millennia.

This occult presence of Orion-Osiris by stellar orientation would have been important because the rites that took place at Luxor Temple symbolized a sort of resurrection of the pharaoh and his Ka. The main axis of the Sanctuary of Amun has an azimuth of about 210–211° and is aligned to the point of last visibility (heliacal setting) of Orion's Belt at its lowest declination, occurring around 10,700 BCE. If we refer to the reciprocal azimuth of 210°, the stellar phenomenon would have occurred behind the temple, and in perfect alignment with it. The ceremonies performed at the sanctuary may have included the famous Opening of the Mouth ritual performed upon the statue of Amun in front of the point of the horizon where Orion's Belt set at its minimum declination.

In the central room of the sanctuary—the one containing the statue of Amun—a diagonal axis follows the direction of the real rising of Sirius at its minimum declination. The same line of Sirius is found in a diagonal axis in the Temple of Sethi at Karnak. The Temple of Seth is yet another famous temple that is oriented to the sunrise at the winter solstice.

In the second part of *Ancient Egypt, Jerusalem and the Stars*, I also explain how and why the principles of this sacred astronomy made Jerusalem the holy city of the Abrahamic religions. More on this in a future article.

Sources & Notes

Albano, Giacomo: *Ancient Egypt, Jerusalem and the Stars: Archaeoastronomical Evidence of a Secret Sacred Astronomy*, 2023.

Albano, Giacomo: *The Journey of the Stars: Tables of minimum and maximum star declinations in the current precessional cycle*, 2023.

1. https://en.wikipedia.org/wiki/Shunet_El_Zebib
2. https://it.wikipedia.org/wiki/Ramesseum#/media/File:S_F-E-CAMERON_EGYPT_2005_RAMASEUM_01320.JPG
3. https://it.wikipedia.org/wiki/File:Abu_Simbel_-_Allerheiligstes.jpg
4. Wikimedia Commons CC BY-SA 3.0.

THEA N. ANDERSON

The Imperial 95: An Astrological Excavation of the History of Convict Leasing in Sugar Land, Texas

If you're ever ever down in Houston,
Boy, you better walk right.
And you better not squabble.
And you better not fight.
Bason and Brock will arrest you.
Payton and Boone will take you down.
You can bet your bottom dollar,
That you're Sugar Land bound.

—*Midnight Special*, Prisoners of the American South (1905) recorded by Lead Belly (1934)

ONE FEBRUARY MORNING IN 2018, a tractor unearthed something strange while back-filling a trench in Sugar Land, Texas. The Fort Bend Independent School District was breaking ground on a trade school at the intersection of Highway 90 and Interstate 6. Not too far off, the dilapidated Imperial Sugar Refinery loomed vacant. It hadn't produced sugar in decades, and real estate developers surrounded its silos like vultures. Sugar Land was awash in new construction and the historic factory stood on the perfect site for a boutique hotel or shopping district.

Archeologists were summoned to the construction site to investigate. Lumped together with prehistoric pottery and fresh-water mussels, were human bone fragments. Construction came to a halt. Time stood still. Over the next several months, dozens of human remains were uncovered—all from the 1800s. All African-American origin. In the end, 94 men and one woman were found having died where they stood. The infamous Hell Hole of the Brazos had been resurrected.

— — —

Eclipses are powerful omens. Just before the discovery of the Imperial 95, eclipses took place that trace a path back to the era when slave labor built one of the country's most prosperous small cities in America. It is a history that had been staunchly denied until that fateful moment in 2018.

First, there was blood on the Moon

The lunar eclipse on January 31st, 2018 laid the astrological groundwork. You may recall this one. At the time, NASA called it a "Super Blue Blood Moon" eclipse—a name as theatrical as the display it presented in North America. Its cosmic fanfare united astronomers and astrologers alike. This eclipse was a spectacle to behold with the Moon at its perigee (the point in its orbit nearest to the Earth), shining significantly brighter than usual. Spectators watched the Moon at dawn on the horizon reflect a blood-tinted shadow.

The charts of eclipses signal new eras, junctures, and political trends. In mundane astrology—that is the astrology of world events—eclipses unveil shadowy beginnings, as well as endings. To the ancients, eclipses were fearsome. Think of how ominous it must have been to have the sovereign Sun or Moon suddenly blotted out. Eclipses came to signify the toppling of reigning authorities, kings, and governments. It is striking that the Imperial Sugar Company's logo and the official seal of Sugar Land both contain a royal crown. These eclipses dug up the truth of the city that had reached great economic prosperity. Its crown was about to slip.

A lunar eclipse happens when the Moon is obscured by the Earth's shadow. In the chart of the January 31st eclipse (Fig. 1), the Sun is on the ascendant at 11° Aquarius. Its face and Egyptian term lord is Mercury: the herald and guide of souls. At 29° Capricorn, Mercury is at an important threshold between traditional frameworks (Capricorn) and new stories (Aquarius).

The Moon, crimson in the dawn sky, is exactly conjunct the minor planet Ceres during the eclipse. Once deemed an asteroid, Ceres orbits between Mars and Jupiter and is the only outer body that has its own gravity. It was promoted from asteroid to minor planet status in 2006 by the International Astronomical Union, the same year that Pluto (planet of the underworld) was demoted from planet to minor planet. The goddess of the harvest and the god of death were suddenly, by name, on equal footing.

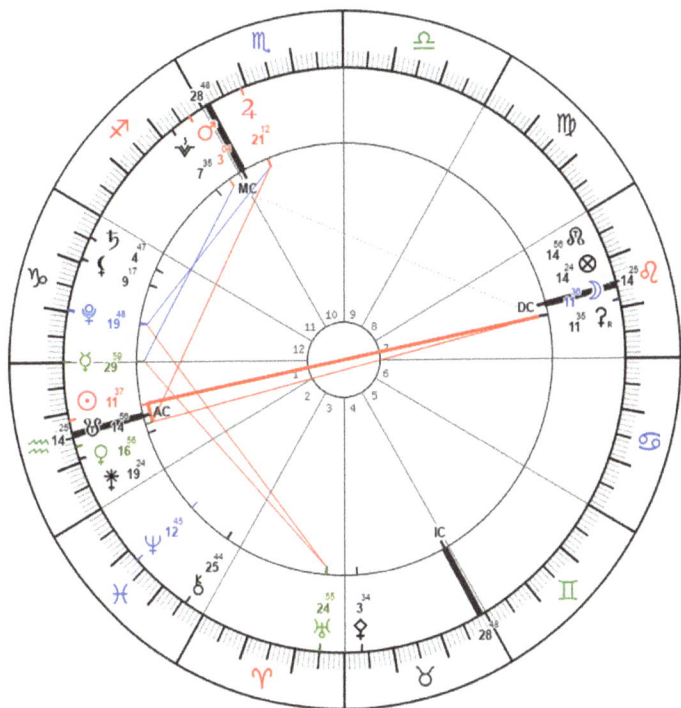

Figure 1: Blood Moon Eclipse on Jan. 31, 2018. Sugar Land, Texas.

Ceres speaks: they were children

Ceres is the goddess of grain, cultivation, harvest, burial, abduction, grief, childbirth, and fertility. In the Blood Moon eclipse chart, Ceres is angular, emphasizing its significance at this moment. This conjunction is a blend of energies between the harvest goddess and the nurturing Moon. It is said that the Moon draws the energy of whatever planetary body it forms an aspect to down to Earth. In Leo, Ceres yearns to be witnessed and acknowledged. By making an exact opposition to the Sun, it confronts the imperialistic power structure that captured people via the convict leasing apparatus.

We know the pain of Ceres. In the myth of the Rape of Persephone, Demeter (Ceres) loses her daughter to Hades (Pluto). Demeter grieved for her lost child and refused to allow any crop to grow. The Earth became barren. No child was born. The Earth, once abundant, became a place of death. Astrologically, Ceres signifies abduction and grief, themes that are central in the story of the Imperial 95—those young men who were returned to the plantation to harvest sugar after slavery had been abolished. As Ceres opposes the Sun—the signifier for the imperialistic, colonial planter class—in the Blood Moon eclipse chart, the minor planet with a sickle-shaped glyph would not be written out of this story.

The chart of the Blood Moon eclipse pointed to where the lost graves of the Imperial 95 were found. The chart's Imum Coeli or IC is conjunct the fixed star Alcyone at 28° Taurus. The IC, is the lowest part of the sky that the planets reach in a 24-hour period and represents internment, burial, death, cemeteries, and family plots. Alcyone is the "inner eye" of the Taurus constellation and the indicator star of the Pleiades—the cluster of seven stars representing seven sisters placed in the bull of the heavens to be protected from the hunter Orion. The star itself reveals what has been occulted or hidden with penetrating intensity.[1] The unmarked cemetery where the Imperial 95 were found— the very graveyard that had eluded local activists for decades—would come to be named the Bullhead Convict Labor Camp. The shocking discovery was made at the head of the Bull of the Heaven.

Forensic archeologists determined that the median age of the Imperial 95 was 24 years old.[2] The youngest of whom was 16-year-old William Nash who died months after entering the labor camp. The vast majority were young Black men, arrested on charges of vagrancy and theft. Claims against them were often falsified. They were often sentenced without proof.

Abysmal conditions, corporal punishment, and cruelty were mainstays at Bullhead, owned and operated by Confederate colonels Edward H. Cunningham and Littleberry A. Ellis. One punishment involved laborers being lowered into a pit in the ground. They would stand shoulder to shoulder. Workers suffocated because of lack of air—some were buried alive. Most of the time, laborers tried to escape

Nash, William 8035	5'4" 151 Black	Cook	GA	No	Theft of property over $20 value	4	19 Apr 1892 McLennan 16 y/o	27 Apr 1892	3 Sept 1893 LAE 16 y/o	Congestion of brain	Ellis Camp number not noted. Died after 8 months on Ellis Camps, not clear which camp. Scars on forehead, left temple, right wrist, small of back. Fourth finger each hand disfigured.
Scott, West 6218	5'1" 147 Dark Mulatto	Farmer	TX	No	Theft	2	5 Mar 1890 Smith 18 y/o	25 Mar 1890	21 July 1890 LAE #1 18 y/o	Killed during escape attempt	Died after 3 months at Ellis Camp #1. Killed while trying to escape by Guard James Clark and hit with 10 (buck)shot. Scars on right temple, right groin, left shoulder blade.

into the woods. Some made it to freedom but most were shot by the patrollers who sat atop high horses with rifles at their sides. The patrollers were a constant presence, and their orders were to shoot at the first sign of a convict's attempt to run.

The most deadly threat to the laborers was yellow fever. Mosquitoes transmitted the disease, passing it from person to person. There was no protection from it. The prisoners were shoeless, ankle-deep in wetlands, arched over the earth as the fever danced between them. They had no access to medical care: Cunningham and Ellis had no incentive to provide it. They knew that laborers who died could be replaced, replenished. The legal arm of convict leasing made sure that a steady stream of Black men were regularly imprisoned and sent to work at the farm.

A solar eclipse changes the dominant narrative

Eclipses happen in pairs, and two weeks later, on February 15th, 2018, a partial solar eclipse in Aquarius took place. The Imperial 95 were discovered just four days later.

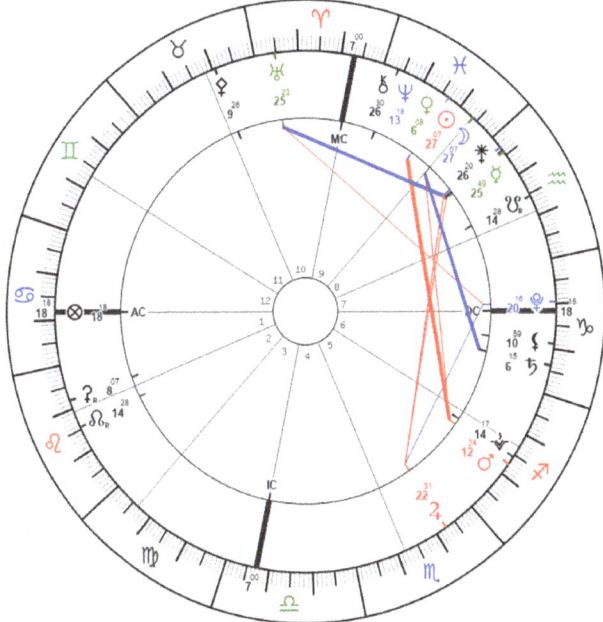

Figure 2: Solar eclipse on February 15th, 2018. Sugar Land, Texas

The February 15th eclipse chart has Cancer rising and the Moon as the chart ruler in the 8th House of death and sacrifice. In its New Moon moment, the planet of nurturing, instinct and memory is in the heart of the Sun in a "dark house" and without its own light. Meanwhile, the Sun is in Aquarius—the sign of its exile—which evokes themes of incarceration and being outside or at the margins of society as those sentenced to convict leasing were. This solar eclipse on the South Node (a point of release and endings) in the 8th House highlights the shadowy inheritances and received legacies that are soon to be revealed and upended. This is particularly true for planets in Aquarius—the fixed air sign—where ideologies and human frameworks about society can lean towards the static and rigid. Those ideals may not yield to change until an eclipse flickers in that sign. As Sugar Land would soon discover, this solar eclipse uncovered hard truths about its history that had been locked away in assumptions and stale narratives that served those in power.

The eclipse chart also includes significations of death, endings, and confinement that speak to the horrors of convict leasing. Ceres is still in Leo and copresent with the North Node in the 2nd house—the house of livelihood and sustenance. Hellenistic astrologers referred to this house as the "Gate of Hades"[3] because of its succedent quality to the 1st house. The 2nd house always rises up to the 1st house, and shows the way to all the houses below the horizon. With the 2nd-house ruler in detriment, and in the 8th house of death, the stories that sustained Sugar Land are soon to be composted so that a newer one can be reborn. In any chart, the 2nd and 8th houses speak to what must be paid.

Death and confinement are also shown in the way that Pluto—the planet of the underworld—is right on the descendant or "the setting place." Saturn in Capricorn, having just set, disposes the solar eclipse in Aquarius prescribing an end and limitation.

Mercury—the herald—is conjunct the solar eclipse at 25° Aquarius and makes it so that the truth will be revealed in a public, paradigm-shifting way.

In many ways, the second eclipse is a reverb of the first in the pair that took place on January 31st. Of the two eclipses, for reasons having to do with proximity to the nodes and visibility on American soil, the January 31st eclipse chart is striking in the way that it speaks to the unearthing of the Imperial 95. The February 15th eclipse highlights the implications of such a revelation.

Together, these two eclipses tell a concordance of meaning: that what happened and the way we choose to tell would become equally important. Remembering the dead, and the spirits of place is how we care for them in and throughout time.

More eclipses and Sugar Land lives out its Uranus return

On July 12, 2018, five months after the January 31st and February 15th eclipses, there was a solar eclipse directly opposite Pluto, planet of the underworld, death, resources, obsession, wealth, and power. The nodes were still in the fixed signs of Leo and Aquarius but this was the first eclipse in a cycle that would see them move into the cardinal signs of Cancer and Capricorn. The switchover in modality was palpable for the lost graves at Sugar Land. Prominent national news outlets suddenly began to write and opine on the convict leasing practice that built the small city following their discovery. Something had been sparked.

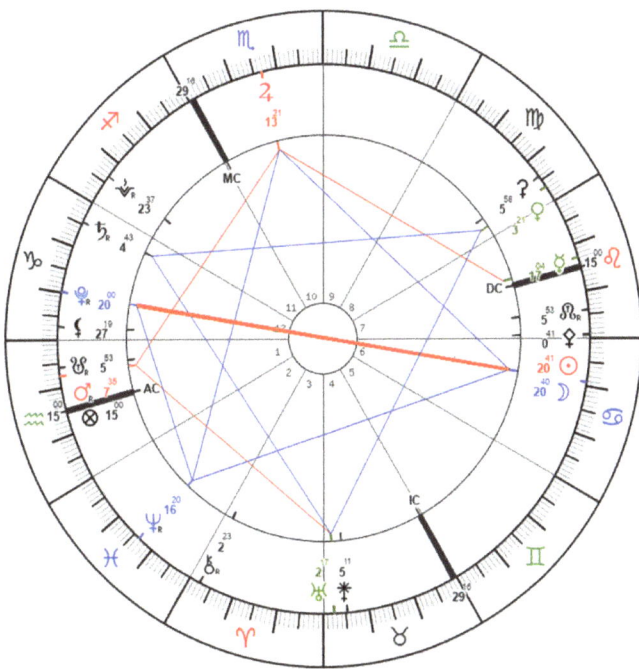

Figure 3: Solar eclipse of July 12, 2018. Sugar Land, TX.

Between January 31st and July 12th, 2018, Mercury had moved from the last degrees of Capricorn to within a few degrees of where the Moon, Ceres, and North Node were huddled in Leo. Mercury relays messages, retrieves souls from the underworld, and heralds information. In Leo, the planet of communication is poised to narrate the story of the enslaved prisoners, their exploitation and previously suppressed legacy.

Just six days after the solar eclipse on July 18, 2018, the *New York Times* ran a piece titled "Remains of Black People Forced Into Labor After Slavery Are Discovered in Texas," announcing that 'the Fort Bend Independent School District is building a technical high school on the site of a former sugar plantation that later served as a state-run prison farm." An archeologist is quoted explaining that the discovery "really does change the history books in Texas."[4] On the same day, the *Washington Post* published a similar piece.

Over the next several months, the discovery would break national news. The story of the Imperial 95 and the history of the unpaid labor that built Sugar Land could no longer be denied. It was a watershed moment for activists like Reginald Moore who had petitioned the government to look for the graves for nearly two decades.

Astrologically, Sugar Land was in a pivotal moment: its Uranus Return. This was the second time Uranus had returned for Sugar Land. The settlement's first Uranus return occurred in 1935, when the Great Depression rocked the refinery and company town that had been built around it. No one expected the demand for refined sugar to decrease the way that it did when food was rationed in that period of history.

In the chart of the Sugar Land Plantation—set for the moment it was named by William J. Kyle and Benjamin Frank Terry who purchased the land on January 1, 1853—Uranus is in the very early degrees of Taurus.[5]

Uranus is the planet of stunning developments, plot twists, and shocking discoveries. The planet of surprises takes 84 years to complete its cycle around all twelve signs of the zodiac. When it approaches its natal degree, wild revelations are in store. This was the case in early 2018, as Uranus began to reapproach its place in the Sugar Land Plantation birth chart.

After the discovery of the Imperial 95, what people knew about the Sugar Land origin story was turned on its head. That only intensified once Uranus moved into Taurus for the first time in seven years from May to November in 2018. The move shattered the narrative that

Figure 4: Image of inmate laborers at Sugar Land, TX. Source: Sugar Land Heritage Foundation.

city officials like then City Manager Allen Bogard, had on record. Just a year prior, in 2017, in an interview with the *Texas Monthly*, Bogard had stated:

> There's not a single facility, road, nor improvement that exists today in the city of Sugar Land that can be traced back to either the convict-lease program or slavery...

Bogard further denied Black contribution to the city of Sugar Land, past and present:

> We have a population that is less than ten percent African American and has never been a significant part of our recent history since we've existed as a city, even though we've had black representatives on our city council on two different occasions. So that is a part of our history... it's nothing that ever comes up here, other than that occasionally we have a conversation with Reginald Moore.[6]

However, once the graves of the convicts were accidentally discovered—on the January 31 and July 12 eclipses with Uranus approaching its natal position—the stunning truth of who built Sugar Land had to be reckoned with.

**Convict leasing: a cruel apparatus after slavery—
Uranus and Pluto square (1878)**

After the Civil War, two Confederate colonels returned to Texas and acquired portions of the Sugar Land Plantation. It was muddy lowland, filled with creeks and wet soil like the Louisiana coast and the Caribbean, where cane production flourished.

After five years, Edward H. Cunningham and Littleberry A. Ellis had amassed enough lowland to establish a cane sugar operation. All they needed was a labor force. At the time, slavery had been abolished for more than a decade. Freedpeople would not sharecrop the dangerous and deadly cane fields rife with Yellow fever and hellish, stifling temperatures. So Cunningham and Ellis concocted a scheme to lease inmates from The Walls prison at Huntsville to work, unpaid, in their labor camp. 78 percent of the inmates died within the operation's first year. The fields were, in essence, death camps.

All of this was completely legal. The 13th Amendment abolished the slavery that America had known. But a covert stipulation left the door open for it to continue in another form.

> Neither slavery nor involuntary servitude, except as punishment for crime, whereof the party shall have been duly convicted, shall exist within the United States, nor any place subject to their jurisdiction.
> —US Constitution. amend. XIII (1865)

The slave labor of inmates resuscitated the Southern economy as slavery continued in its new form. During Cunningham's reign at Sugar Land, 633 convicts died and 1,151 escaped. It was a notorious, hellish operation. Before the city of Sugar Land would become one of the most prosperous small cities in the United States, it was known as the Hell Hole of the Brazos: a gaping, mosquito-infested, gator-patrolled mouth of Hades worked by enslaved convicts.

Pluto manifests at Sugar Land: The Texas King of Sugar contracts with the state to lease convicts

They called Edward H. Cunningham the Texas King of Sugar or the Colonel, depending on the day. His kingship was earned by manufacturing sugar cane and waging war. Both endeavors resulted in death, imprisonment, and suffering so profound they've made a mark on history. Cunningham was Hades, a Plutonian figure who "dressed in black, with a wide-brimmed hat to match...resplendent with a great diamond stud."[7] His appetite for food and spirits was unrivaled, except perhaps by his appetite for money.

> *If we invest...then the state of Texas shall experience a boon such that it has never seen. And money, I assume is why we're all here.* —Cunningham in the *San Francisco Gazette* (giving a tour of the Imperial Sugar Mill.)

Cunningham and Ellis submitted a bid to the state of Texas to lease prisoners that was granted on January 1, 1878.[8] In the chart of the moment that the Cunningham & Ellis convict leasing contract went into effect, Uranus was squaring Pluto (Fig. 5). Uranus—the planet of mavericks and wayward thinkers—was retrograde, conjunct the South Node (one of the Moon's eclipsing points), and at the final degree of Leo. This configuration highlights the shadowy side of the Uranian archetype that exploits its genius to come up with schemes for self-fulfilling needs, instead of seeking freedom (Uranus at 29 Leo). When Cunningham & Ellis took over the failed Wayward & Dewy lease, they promised to repair the convict leasing system and make it "more humane". But as history would come to reveal, the lease was a scheme to continue slavery and enrich the plantation owners yet again.

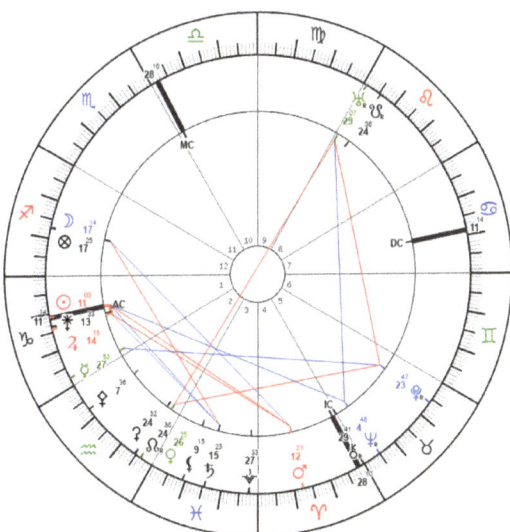

Figure 5: The 1878 Convict Lease Contract between Cunningham & Ellis and the State of Texas.[9]

The Reconstruction Era was rife with challenges to freedom in a world still overseen by the people who established American slavery and benefited from its exploitation. The waxing square, where Uranus moves to a 90° angle with Pluto, displays the struggle between freedom and oppression that was ongoing in the years following the Civil War and Emancipation. The Northern states were fatigued of managing Southern affairs, giving way for political pressure and business interests to give agency back to the Southern landed gentry class. The retrograde motion of Uranus (innovation) and Pluto (resources), highlights a struggle to return to old ways of maintaining power and working the land. With Pluto at the North Bending (a point that can symbolize a skipped step or unchecked desire), the hunger for land, money in their Taurean significations was at a new peak. During the 1870s, policies like the Black Codes saw free Black people arrested for crimes such as vagrancy, standing on grass, or stealing food. The Black Codes established a new paradigm for exploiting unpaid Black labor. If there was a labor shortage, then arrests for Black Code felonies rose. Professional crime hunters searched for "felons." It didn't matter if the person arrested was found guilty or not. If they couldn't pay their court fees, then they were sent to the farm. Black people without proof of work were deemed "idle" and were sent to the farm, too.

This new pipeline siphoned convicts to Cunningham's Imperial Sugar farm. The chart's Uranus-Pluto square in fixed signs, with both planets retrograde, shows the power structure's grip on the way things used to be during chattel slavery. Cunningham would come to preside over the biggest convict lease system in the United States with over 2,000 convicts at its peak—most of whom were formerly enslaved.

As W. E. B. Du Bois writes in *Black Reconstruction in America* (1935): "The slave went free; stood a brief moment in the Sun; then moved back again toward slavery."

**Upending of an old narrative for Sugar Land—
as fated in the eclipse and Uranus' return**

In the first grade, my class went on a field trip to tour the Imperial Sugar Refinery. The tour guide led our class to a balcony inside the Char House (named for the use of powdered or "char" animal bones in the refining process in the 1800s) where we overlooked the spectacle of machinery. Monstrous tractors shoveled white and brown sugar—coarse and refined—separating sucrose in its different phases. Metal groaned. Fermentation's sweet rot smacked our faces. An employee, definitely unacquainted with children, distributed packets of table sugar that we promptly ripped open and threw back like shots. The place had been a let-down (as these places often are) but something about it was haunting. Mounted on the historical wall, I noticed a framed black and white photograph of the farm workers in front of large looming stalks of sugarcane. They were all Black men, wearing prison stripes, somber in expression, staring off somewhere beyond the camera. As one of the few Black children in my class, I was entranced, curious, and ashamed.

The Imperial 95 were reinterred on November 27, 2019. This point in time coincided with the era when Saturn in Capricorn was drawing closer to Pluto in Capricorn with the South Node present. It was a period of reckoning for the United States as unmarked graves belonging to those of African-American ancestry were discovered. That same month, archaeologists discovered Ridgewood Cemetery: a segregation-era cemetery. In December 2019, a mass grave from the 1921 Tulsa Race Massacre in Oklahoma was discovered. Mass graves were found under apartment complexes, parking lots and other built-over places. In a 2021 *New Yorker* article, writer Jill Lepore proclaimed that '[u]nderneath America lies an apartheid of the departed. Violence done to the living is usually done to their dead...'[10]

In the five years since the Imperial 95 were discovered, there is still debate about what should be done. How do we memorialize those who perished laboring on the prison farm to build the town of Sugar Land? What does restorative justice look like for the descendants of convicts? As Uranus continues to travel through Taurus, the nation has had to ask questions about Tauruean significations like internment, land, and resources. The Nodes touring through Scorpio and Taurus unearthed these histories. And now, with the Nodes in Aries and Libra starting July 2023, archeologists, researchers, and activists are asking the question: What does restorative justice look like for Black descendants?

This year, Ashanté Reese wrote about the intergenerational impact of the Imperial 95 for the *Washington Post*:

> The incarceration of so many Black people during the era of the Black Codes therefore deeply influenced their loved ones, even as it provided the labor that laid the foundation for Sugar Land eventually to become one of the richest cities in the United States.[11]

As the local school district writes an executive summary, updates the curriculum, and as the City creates a memorial to the convicts—streets still bear Cunningham's name. The Imperial 95 are still marked as "unknown" in plaques on the ground as students filter in and out of the technical school. The local Marriot hotel displays a copper vat over which enslaved people labored to refine sugar. It was the unpaid labor of Black men and women that separated scum from molasses to refine sugar, enriched Cunningham, Ellis and others, and gave the city of Sugar Land its economic start.

Astrology pierces the veil of historical narratives. The eclipses in the winter of 2018 pointed to where the Imperial 95 were buried after a century of being lost. Sugar Land's Uranus return coincided with convict leasing making national news, ushering in a total paradigm shift. As the news circulated, I remember seeing the photograph of convicts in the refinery. With this insistent memory, I asked questions and pulled charts.

As a tireless grassroots activist, the late Reginald Moore knew for decades what the eclipse charts signified: that omission always points to what is omitted. As a first grader, I knew it too. And sure enough, the story of those ensnared in convict leasing at Sugar Land to enrich Edward Cunningham and the like would have to be reckoned with. The eclipse in January 2018 showed us the way to the truth of slave capital at Sugar Land. Astrology is time, illustrated. And it was only a matter of time until the Hell Hole of the Brazos would rise up to meet Sugar Land.

Notes:

1. Brady, Bernadette, *Star and Planet Combinations* (Bournemouth: Wessex Astrologer, 2008), 88.
2. "Honoring the Sugar Land 95." *Fort Bend Independent School District*.
3. Paulus Alexandrinus, 4th century CE; and Vettius Valens, 2nd century CE.
4. Sarah Mervosh, "Remains of Black People Forced into Labor after Slavery Are Discovered in Texas," *The New York Times*, 2018.
5. Cities, states, and countries can have several birth charts: For Sugar Land, the story begins with the Karwankara First People who inhabited the land along the Gulf part of Texas. In the 1800s, Stephen F. Austin arrived with the Old 300—the first Black enslaved people forcibly moved from the eastern seaboard of the US because Austin promised that slavery would continue in Texas. The 1959 formal town incorporation is another possibility for the

inception chart. But there is something about a place first being named, uttered into the world, that speaks to its fate and legacy. This January 1st, 1853 date is the root of the story of Sugar Land as it was conceived for the refining of sugar cane by unpaid labor through American slavery and then convict leasing.

6. Michael Hardy, "Blood and Sugar," *Texas Monthly*, 2017.
7. Robert Perkinson, *Texas Tough: The Rise of America's Prison Empire* (London: Picador, 2010), 84.
8. "Fear, Force, and Leather: the Texas Prison System's First Hundred Years, 1848–1948," Texas State Library and Archives Commission, 2019.
9. Untimed chart. Houses derived from the Sun.
10. Jill Lepore, "When Black History Is Unearthed, Who Gets to Speak for the Dead?" *The New Yorker*, 2021.
11. Ashanté Reece, "A History of Unfree Labor Haunts Us," *Washington Post*, 2023.

DREW LEVANTI

Satellite

The satellite sags heavy on the starry night,
cold lens fixed on the surface

They say it was just this way,
the day we came from the sky

When our feathery feet touched
down printlessly in the damp dirt

And we taught the trees
the ancient tongues, chanted
the universal vowels, mouths
bound open to the coursing swill of stars

O heavenly intelligences,
orbiting oblivion, sky scraping seers

Metal, mind, myth
Spawn of Sputnik

Relinquish the potionhold of this amnesia
Grow toes of devotion

Dance amid
the fingerling fog

Tremble as the ground
remembering our rhythm,

and listen as the land
joins in palimpsest song

and we feast on the salt
of our alchemy

So it is
I can feel the spirits

grazing the back of my neck
saying yes

Yes, nature will take back
the cities, cover over

concrete blankets with moss, drape
lichen from steel, braid
vines with barbed
wire, carbon round carbon, double
helix, nucleic nectar,
elixir of life

For the gleam of gold
my ancestors buried lakes beneath broken ships,

reversed rivers,
heaved water up mountains,

the empire's
height, tired,

glacial aging, my humbling
birthright is to descend

settle like sand
melt like the sugar of moonlight

feel the falling grace of gravity
and accept the oceancall of home

ANNE C. SCHNEIDER

Relocating the Solar Return Chart
A Report from Practical Experience

For many years I have been choosing my travel destinations not so much based on the climate, the season, or the charm of a place, but rather according to astrological criteria: I keep trying to use the change of location to mitigate or overcome difficult positions in solar and lunar return charts. If I change my location on my solar or lunar birthday, I can reposition the angles of the horoscope. While I cannot change the positions of the planets in the signs and their aspects to each other, I can avoid critical factors, such as having disharmonious aspects on the angles and making sure traditionally difficult houses (such as 6, 8 and 12) are not heavily occupied. Beyond such a "limitation of potential damage," I can also focus on getting the benefics and other positive factors into a favourable place or, specifically strengthen and emphasize houses relevant for a certain purpose. This exercise will theoretically result in a choice between different geographical areas or places: It is rare for just one single location or a small geographical area to present itself as ideal. More often several choices are suitable—with different emphasis on specific horoscope houses and gradual weighting of positive impact.

From a purely astrological point of view, a short stay of less than an hour at the exact moment of the solar or lunar return at the exact minute would be sufficient to achieve this goal—according to practical experience. But I personally like to take the opportunity of such a relocation to stay in one place for longer and explore it in more detail, especially if it was previously unknown to me. This has taken me to the most unusual places that I would probably never have visited without this technique. These trips are not always comfortable! This method has had me take trips to Baku (Azerbaijan), Porto Alegre (Brazil), Pegu (Myanmar). Several times I had to get close to the Arctic Circle in Scandinavia, or make my way to the Azores in stormy weather. As challenging as they may have been, they were all definitely worth it.

Part of the metaphysical experience of this "cosmic manipulation" is to go through this process of geographical approaching.

As a Sagittarius with a Sun-Jupiter conjunction, I consider myself as a perpetual wanderer anyway, and I don't see these journeys as a burden, but as an expansion of my horizon.

Clients, who I advise in this regard, understandably do not want to be sent to a remote place, such as a South Sea island, Greenland, or Kamchatka, where it takes a lot of effort to get there. They would rather spend a relaxing holiday somewhere, where you can also experience a good solar relocation, among other things. This approach fails to demonstrate an adequate perspective and set of priorities. The far-sighted planning of the solar return trip—or, ideally, several solar returns in a sequence—should take precedence over pure holiday fun, when planning your life with the help of astrological insight. A quiet, healthy year afterwards that supports the achievement of a certain goal usually makes up for the trouble of having to get to a remote place.

Restrictions on freedom of travel can also arise again and again: Many astrologically suitable destinations are difficult or not accessible at all for political reasons, and in some professions, one cannot spend too much time away at any given moment. Pragmatic considerations will heavily influence the choice of location. During the COVID-19 pandemic, certain places were unreachable without a special resourcefulness and great courage. I know a few wonderful stories about this from the circles of my teacher and mentor, Ciro Discepolo. More than any other astrologer who practises and perfects this technique, he has crystallized and systematized the rules to be observed, using a huge sample of more than 20,000 horoscopes from family, clients, and public figures and has written numerous books (with translations into many languages) published on this. Some of these sources are available for free on his website.[1]

Methodical Issues and Approach

There are different schools of thought regarding the calculation of the solar horoscope: one, including Vedic astrology, says that the place of birth should always be used when calculating the solar return chart (Vedic: Varshaphala), but others postulate the respective location where the native stays on his solar return day. Now it is clear that historically, at the time the technique of the solar revolution was developed, people did not usually travel far enough to cause significant changes in the horoscope angles, let alone in the house positions of the planets.

The astronomer and astrologer Jean Baptiste Morin (1583–1656) is one of the first to calculate his own and others' solar return charts based on the place of residence and not on the place of birth in his *Astrologica gallica, Book 23*—but these are mostly retrospective considerations and not forward-looking advice to clients.[2] However, over many years of practice, using his own horoscope and that of his employers and clients, he had discovered that he could make better predictions about the course of the year based on the relocated solar return chart than on that based on the place of birth. I bring up Morin's position as an important methodological point of view, even if it originally had nothing to do with optimizing the solar return chart via travel.

The following procedure is recommended in practice: First, calculate the basic solar return (using Placidus houses) for the native's usual place of residence. Check it for poor house placements (planets in 6,8,12) and disharmonious aspects on the angles. If critical positions speak against staying at the usual place of residence, project the solar return chart onto a world map using Astro*carto*graphy. Look for suitable, favorable planetary lines—especially Jupiter on MC/AC/DC or Sun on MC. Then erect a complete solar return chart for the significant places shown on these lines. This may require travel to remote locations. Sometimes there are simply no accessible optimal locations as the most suitable ones are in the middle of the ocean! If a very good location cannot be reached, it is better to limit the damage than do nothing at all. A "compromise place" should be sought that prevents the worst impediment.

If a specific event or goal is the focus of a solar year (e.g., job change, partnership, opening a business, health, operation, etc.), the corresponding solar house should be strengthened. Positive planets and benefics should be located there, but no malefics. Besides, the solar return AC shall also fall into a suitable house of the natal chart. To further fine-tune the event/goal, you can go to the lunar return level, and select the most appropriate lunar return for the event. Let's now look at a few examples, which help to clarify the theory:

An Example: Realignment of Professional Life

In 2018, I planned to leave my full-time job as an editorial project manager in the US IT industry to devote more time to astrology, travel, and other interests. As part of restructuration measures, my company had repeatedly launched severance pay programs in order to reduce the workforce and thus make the per capita profit appear more attractive to their shareholders. That's what I was hoping for, even though around my birthday at the end of 2017 nothing of the kind was announced for the time of my planned exit (on the second Saturn Return). Thus, it was important to me to position the issue of "career" well in Solar Return chart 2017, but without running the risk of provoking other negative "side effects" in other areas.

Calculated for Mainz, Germany, where I live, a critical constellation appeared in the solar return chart, namely Mars-Uranus opposed directly on the AC-DC axis (Fig. 1). Such an aspect signals accidents and potential dangers to health and should be avoided at all costs. In addition, all the planets were below the horizon, which would certainly not be conducive to favorable career options. Thus, to move the majority of planets to the upper hemisphere I would have to travel halfway around the world. An astro-cartographic view of my solar return showed a Jupiter-MC line coursing across the Far East, roughly on the border between Thailand and Southern Myanmar (Fig. 2, next page). Luckily, I had wanted to visit Myanmar for a long time, so I decided to spend my birthday there. Now, I had to determine the exact location.

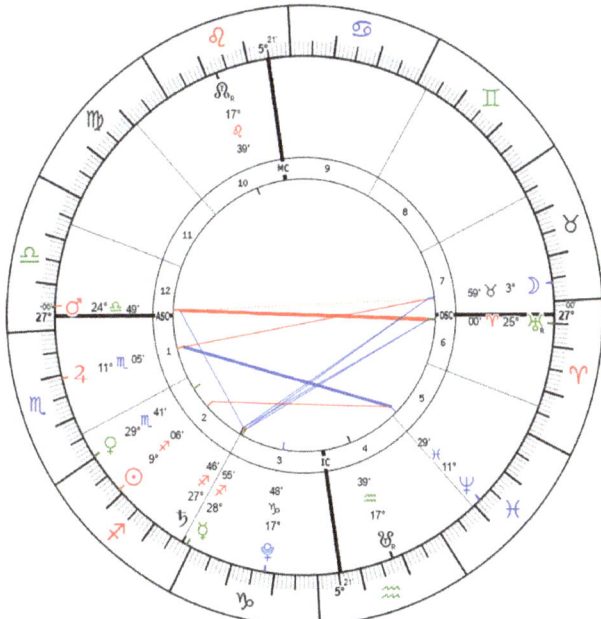

Figure 1: My solar return cast for 2017. Rodden rating AA: BC in hand.

Figure 2: My solar return for 2017, mapped using Solar Fire 9.

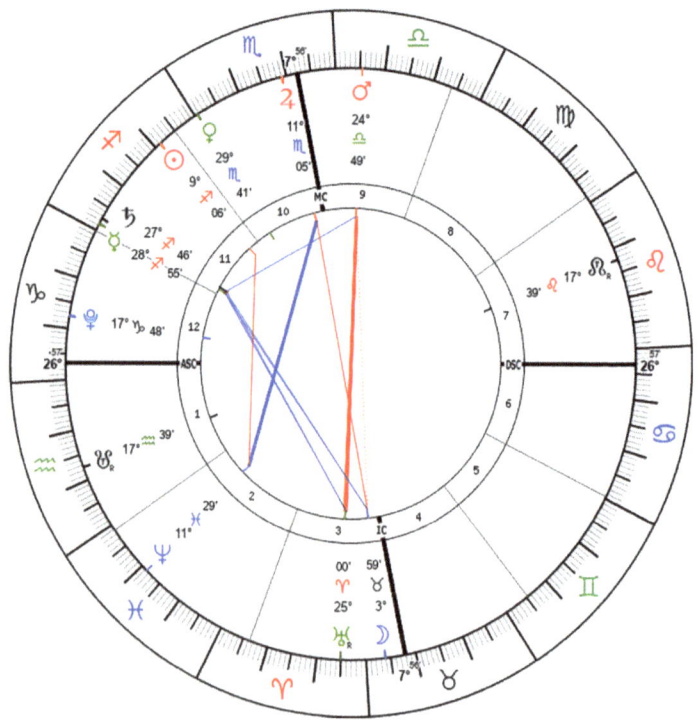

Figure 3: My solar return relocated to Golden Rock for 2017.
Rodden rating AA: BC in hand.

For the Burmese capital Yangoon, my Solar Return Jupiter was already close to the Solar Return MC (within 2.5°), which in itself would be sufficient for the planned effect. A little further Southeast it would come even closer. Conveniently, the Golden Rock, one of the three main Buddhist shrines in Myanmar, was located close to the site of the exact conjunction—in the middle of an extensive, dense forest area (Fig. 3). In this environment, this was the only possibility of a reachable place. But this pilgrimage destination is not so easy to get to—private cars are not allowed, and buses only go to the nearest bigger city. Thus, I hired a driver and a guide, who brought me as close as possible. For the last 16 km I could have either made a pilgrimage on foot through the forest or been rocked up along winding roads to the mountain top crammed on the loading area of a truck together with other pilgrims. Since it was already afternoon when I arrived at the foot of the mountain and it would be dark in a few hours, I decided to take the truck. The sheer beauty of the place made all that effort worth it: at dusk, the "Golden Rock" radiated an indescribably mystical atmosphere in the middle of a wide, wooded and uninhabited mountain panorama.

In addition to the favorable Jupiter position on the Solar Return MC, the relocated solar return chart showed other positive features. Venus was also in the 10th house, which is certainly positive for future professional activities, promising goodwill and a friendly professional atmosphere. The Sun and a strong line-up of planets in the 11th house favor windfalls, i.e., positive things that often fall into your lap without much effort. The solar return AC falls in the natal 4th house, which is also unproblematic. This factor addresses themes of domesticity and family. With the withdrawal from a company environment into freelance work from my desk at home, that's quite fitting. And last, but not least, the critical Mars-Uranus opposition falls into the cadent houses 3 and 9, where, according to the classical interpretation, it has the least impact.

With some insistence on my part in my company, everything finally worked out as I had imagined, and I was able to leave my office job on March 31, 2018—at an exact conjunction of transit Mars and Saturn on my natal IC. I even got my desired severance payment. One Saturn cycle had closed and at the same time Mars had initiated an impulse for a new beginning. I haven't regretted taking this step for a minute.

Another Example: Missed Chances— without Solar Return Relocation

A close friend—who happens to also be skeptical of astrology—told me at the beginning of 2015 that he was planning a trip to the Canary Islands in the spring. I looked at his solar return chart at his place of residence in Germany and found that it showed critical health factors and a risk of accidents. The solar return AC fell into the natal 6th house (chart not shown) and the precise conjunction of Mars and Uranus, which also received a precise square from Pluto, fell on the cusp of the 6th house in the solar return. That didn't bode well.

Based on previous discussions about astrology with him, I didn't expect him to be particularly interested in my advice on how he could actively influence the new year of life for the better. I still tried to explain the potential dangers to him, but I had no success. He simply replied laconically that I was wasting my time on him and on astrology in general. Nothing to be done!

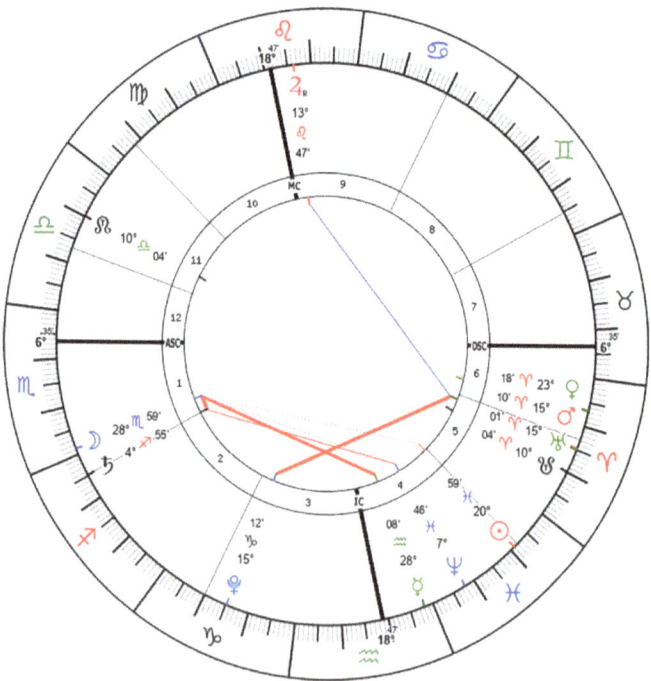

Figure 4: My friend's solar return for 2015. Birthdata withheld for confidentiality. Rodden rating AA: BC in hand.

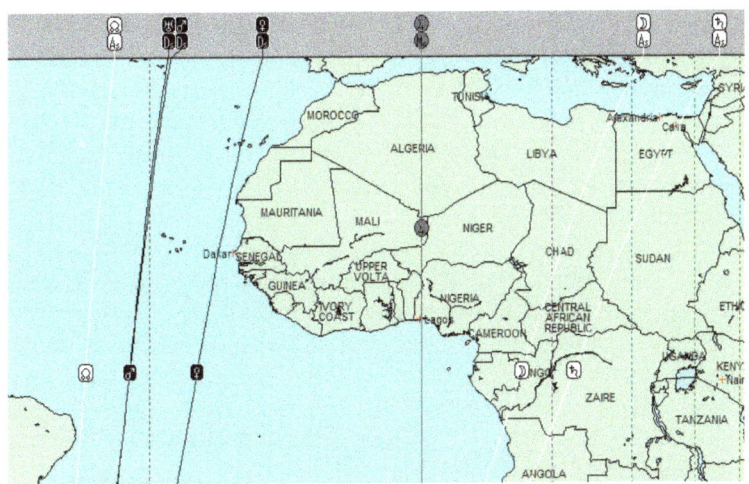

Figure 5: My friend's solar return for 2015, mapped using Solar Fire 9.

As planned, he flew to the Canary Islands in April, a few weeks after his birthday. He had really chosen the most challenging geography to his health for this solar year. The map shows that the archipelago east of the three DC lines of Mars, Uranus and Venus is situated exactly in the zone of the 6th house.

About two weeks later, my friend called me and told me that he had a serious accident in the Canary Islands. He rented a bike that did not have a coaster brake, which he was not used to. On a steep descent he tried to brake but could not control the bike, and he flew upside down over the handlebars. He fell on his face and injured himself and broke his right arm—and his glasses. The accident forced him to cut his trip short. He flew back home to have his injuries and fractures treated in a German hospital.

The lunar return chart of March 23, 2015—with Saturn at the cusp of the 6th house and square to Neptune—shows very clearly that the topic of bones would be addressed in terms of threats to health. In addition, Neptune on the MC of the lunar return symbolizes the longer absence from his job that was required for him to heal.

None of this surprised me at all, but I still couldn't dispel my friend's scepticism towards astrology with this solar forecast. Afterwards, I was curious to find which solar location could possibly have been remedied these events? I took another look at this solar return on the map, and came across the New Orleans area of Louisiana (chart not shown). There the critical Mars-Uranus conjunction moved to the cadent 9th house, where it would have had less impact on his health. The solar return AC moved to the 4th house here, which is not critical for health issues. Pluto strengthened the MC with its trine, and Neptune moved away from the axes. Jupiter, as a benefactor, would have protected the AC as well. Unfortunately, this remains hypothetical, since he did not spend his solar return in New Orleans. We'll never know what could have happened...

In my estimation, to really compare different options, one would have to make observations on biological or astrological twins who spend their solar birthday in different places. Otherwise, one can only write up a solar return forecast for the normal place of residence and for the chosen solar return location in advance, and then compare what happened during the year with this written forecast once the solar year is over. To further explore this way of working with solar (and lunar) returns, I recommend Ciro Discepolo's book *Transits and Solar Returns: A New System of Analysis for Two Ancient Methods*.[4] It is a comprehensive work of reference on all possible planetary positions in the solar return chart including a section of detailed examples. Another example from my own practice was published in the magazine *Meridian* in 2020 and is available online.[5]

Notes:

This article has been adapted from the original German version which appeared in *Meridian* in 2023. All charts use True Node and Placidus Houses.

1. In his complete bibliography, free downloads are marked in turquoise. www.cirodiscepolo.it/biblio.htm
2. Jean-Baptiste Morin, *Astrologica Gallica, Book Twenty-Three, Revolutions*, translated from Latin by James Herschel Holden, 2nd rev. (Tempe, AZ: AFA, 2002).
3. Pictures of this (and other) solar return trips can be watched in Ciro Discepolo's *Aimed Solar Returns*, Vol. I, (Naples, 2009), p. 89, available online: www.cirodiscepolo.it/download/AimedSolarReturnsAShortAlbum.pdf
4 Ciro Discepolo, *Transits and Solar Returns: A New System of Analysis for Two Ancient Methods* (Naples, 2007).
5 Anne C. Schneider, "Die Integration von Radix und Elektionshoroskopen," *Meridian* 2020/2: https://sternwerkstatt.de/artikel/202-20/

GRAY CRAWFORD

Pole Star Epochs: From the Dragon to the Bear

NORTH STAR AND LODESTAR, POLARIS is a guiding light placed at the pivot around which the stars of the northern hemisphere rotate. Ever present at the north celestial pole as we endlessly whirl around Earth's rotational axis, Polaris is as constant as Ananke and her spindle around which the starry spheres spin. Never rising nor setting, Polaris traces a tight circle in the sky due to its proximity to the pole. From Earth, it seems rooted in its central spot like a World Tree or Axis Mundi. On the tail of the Little Bear, Polaris—and the stars of the Great Bear who ceaselessly rotate around the pole star's central position—, has served as a navigational guide for sailors journeying to distant lands by sea and slaves escaping to freedom in the North. We have become so accustomed to seeing Polaris at the dead center of the night sky that we imagine that it has always been there. But this has not always been the case.

In fact, in the roughly 26,000 years it takes the Earth to complete its axial wobble, the north celestial pole slowly circumambulates around the sky. In some eras, there is no visible star at its central northern position. Roughly 14,000 years ago, Vega in the Lyra constellation served as the pole star. More recently—5,000 years ago—Thuban in Draco the Dragon served its tenure. Thuban was the pole star when the Great Pyramids of Egypt were built, claiming its status from approximately 3942 to 1793 BC. Thuban's position as a pole star was especially notable because of its exact presence on the northern celestial pole in approximately 2787 BC. There is only one other visible star that comes close to the exactness of Thuban within the 26,000 year cycle: Polaris. By the end of this century—around 2100 AD—we will experience Polaris at its closest proximity to the pole. It is the only star besides Thuban to be so exactly placed there. We are at an incredibly unique time in the Earth's axial precession, one that will only intensify during the century ahead.

Due to rapid advancements in AI technology, and other factors, there is a growing collective sense that we are living during a transitional time of immense change and uncertainty that has resonance with an epochal turning. In the 20th century, C. G. Jung brought attention to the idea that epochs of time are defined by the constellational stars that align with the Aries equinox when he explored the rise of Christianity and its associated fish symbolism against the backdrop of the shift from the Age of Aries into the Age of Pisces. Before the atomic bombs of the 1940s, Jung predicted the decade would be important due to the astronomer Rebekka Aleida Biegel's claim that the equinoctial point would reach a midpoint between the last star of the Pisces constellation and the first star of the Aquarius constellation in 1940. Biegel calculated that two different stars within Aquarius would align with the equinoctial point in 2129 and 2245. In a footnote in *Aion*, Jung gave a broad range of 1997 to 2154 for the shift into the Age of Aquarius, stating that the exact calculation would depend upon methodology, as well as which stars associated with Aquarius were seriously considered. The important point here though is Jung's emphasis on precessional alignments with fixed stars, and the living symbolism of their constellational imagery. More recently, Robert Hand has drawn from the same idea to demarcate epochs based upon precessional alignments with the Capricorn Solstice. He notes the importance of our shift away from stars in Sagittarius into our present alignment with stars in Ophiuchus, the Serpent Bearer.

In *Babylonian Star Lore*, Gavin White theorized that Babylonian astrologers probably connected the changing position of the pole star with the turning of great epochs, similar to our contemporary ideas about the vernal equinox shifting from Pisces to Aquarius. White wrote that Babylonian astrologers called the circumpolar star region the "Exalted Temple," revealing the importance they gave to the area of the sky that held the axis of the heavens. Although Babylonian astrologers knew that Thuban marked the Exalted Temple in their own time, they were aware that Polaris would eventually claim the title: they called it the "Inheritor of the Exalted Temple." Due to Draco's prominence at the center of the exalted circumpolar region for so long, it is fascinating to consider the central importance of Tiamat, the great chaotic serpent goddess, in Babylonian mythology.

In China, Thuban reached the exact north celestial point around 2787 BC, which aligned with the reign of the Yellow Dragon: the legendary Emperor Hungdi who was said to have begun his rule around 2697–98 BC. Hungdi presided over a Golden Age, and was said to have introduced gifts of civilization such as writing, lunar calendars, wooden homes, and new transportation methods like carts and boats to his people. He was seen as the "Yellow Deity with Four Faces," each face representing the central unity of all four directions, similar to the symbolism of a pole star. After his death, the Yellow Emperor was said to have become an immortal dragon who ascended to the heavens above.

It is interesting that so many cultures around the world, like those of Yoruba people and certain aboriginal tribes in Australia, portray serpents as creator deities or give great prominence to serpentine deities such as the Naga in India. After Thuban began fading away from its central proximity as a pole star in 1793 BC, another dragon star (Kappa Draconis) became an approximate pole star until roughly 1100 BC when another transition began. At this time Kochab in Ursa Minor began vying for pole star status, although it never came nearly as close to the northern celestial pole as Thuban did. The transition out of what appears to be an Age of Dragons began around this time, although some cultures viewed Ursa Minor as the wings of the Dragon and so might have continued connecting it with serpentine imagery. The *MUL.APIN*, which was compiled during this transitional time (around 1000 BC), depicted Ursa Minor as being one of the two Wagons of Heaven (Ursa Major being the other), with the ropes of the wagons bridging heaven and earth.

Thales of Miletus, who lived from approximately 626 to 545 BC, has been credited with naming Ursa Minor and recommending its use as a navigational constellation for due north. Although there was no exact pole star during this era, Ursa Minor would have been clearly moving into a central position as Draco was fading away. By the time Aratus wrote his legendary text *Phaenomena* in roughly 276 BC, Ursa Minor was not only described as possessing the greatest value as a celestial cynosure for the straightest course in navigation, it was also called "Cynosura" drawing on its connection with one of the nymphs who nursed Zeus on Mount Ida. Aratus named Ursa Major after Helike, the other nymph who raised Zeus. The birth of Zeus announced a new era of Olympian gods who would overcome the old gods ruled by Cronus. Importantly, one version of the story directly linked the constellations of Draco, Ursa Minor, and Ursa Major with this epochal shift. It was said that when Cronus was searching for the infant Zeus on Crete to destroy him, Zeus hid himself by transforming into a serpent (drakōn) while also transforming his two nurses into bears. Thus the circumpolar stars took on the identity of the progenitors of the new Olympian Age.

But what exactly does a slow shift from an Age of Dragons to an Age of Bears signify? In *Bear Doctors: Tracing the History of Bears as Healers and how they became Christian Saints*, Roslyn Frank documented an archaic belief amongst people from Basque country in the Pyrenean region, that humans descended from bears. There are other cultures around the world who have believed in an ancestral link between humans and bears, too. The link seems justified by bears' ability to walk upright on two feet, their similar anatomy, intelligence, and dexterity, and our shared omnivorous diets and "sweet tooths." Some believe humans could have learned some traditional medicine from observing bears self-medicate with plants. Potent healing abilities as well as resurrective capacities were ascribed to bears due to their cyclical hibernation. Could there be a connection here between the increasing importance of Polaris and Ursa Minor approaching the north celestial pole?

The pole shift from dragons and snakes to the bear/human is clear within the development of Abrahamic religions through stories like that of Adam, Eve, and the serpent. Many deities, like the Greek Zeus and the Mesopotamian Marduk, took on an anthropomorphized appearance. Human domination over serpents features greatly in both of their stories: Zeus slaying the serpentine Typhon and Marduk splitting the great serpent Tiamat in half, creating the heavens and the earth out of her body. The Islamic tradition has taught that Allah created the jinn before he created Adam. Jinn were thought to be able to take—and had a preference for—serpent form. Indeed, it's common today to hear our world described as an anthropocene, an epoch of time dominated by the impact of humans.

By the time that Pico della Mirandola wrote his *Oration on the Dignity of Man* in 1486, a text that has been linked with the wider collective movement to center humans above all other beings, Polaris had moved much closer to the northern celestial pole and had become the pole star. Mirandola wrote that the "nature of all other beings is limited and constrained within the bounds of laws prescribed," while humans in contrast can set the limits of their own nature through the desires of their free will (cited in *Cosmos and Psyche*, 4). In the 20th century, humans developed atomic power and unleashed the atomic bomb as Polaris came even closer to the pole than it had been. Today, as Polaris is coming even closer to the exact pole position, humanity is rapidly developing artificial intelligence at such speed that questions of a looming AI singularity have grasped the collective imagination.

Rather than continue on a path of further separation from nature, perhaps our ancestral roots in the animal world could point toward a rebalancing taking place in a more animistic direction. The central premise behind Robert Hand's exploration of the Capricorn solstice aligning with the stars in Ophiuchus' serpent-holding-hand is that the centralization of these stars indicates the critical necessity of humanity coming to terms with their consumption and control of the natural world, or risk destroying themselves through ecological disasters and crises. Similarly, Jung associated the transition from the Age of Pisces to Aquarius as being extremely perilous with vast potential for humanity to self-destruct. As the Aries equinox continues to move toward eventual alignment with Aquarius, the most human of all the zodiac signs, perhaps there is a convergence of focus on the human in the century ahead that will demand responsibility and usher in a rebalanced relationship between us and the world around us. One thing is clear: Polaris will be getting even closer to the north celestial pole in the century ahead.

Sources

Eratosthenes and Hyginus Constellation Myths with Aratus's Phaenomena. A new translation by Robin Hand. (2015). Oxford University Press.

Frank, Roslyn. (2022). Bear Doctors: Tracing the History of Bears as Healers and How they became Christian Saints.

Greene, Liz. (2018). Jung's Studies in Astrology: Prophecy, Magic, and the Qualities of Time. Routledge.

Hand, Robert. (2014). The Precession of the Capricorn Solstice and the Importance of 2017 to Humanity. The Mountain Astrologer. October/November 2014 issue.

Jung, C.G. (1981). Aion: Researches into the Phenomenology of the Self. Routledge. Fifth edition.

McLure, Bruce. "Thuban was pole star for the Ancient Egyptians." Earthsky, 9 August 2023, https://earthsky.org/brightest-stars/thuban-past-north-star/

Ogden, Daniel (2013). Drakon: Dragon Myth and Serpent Cult in the Greek and Roman Worlds. Oxford University Press. p. 164

Tarnas, Richard. (2007). Cosmos and Psyche. Plume.

"Thales of Miletus." Wikimedia Foundation, last modified 29 September 2023, https://en.wikipedia.org/wiki/Thales_of_Miletus

White, Gavin. (2007). Babylonian Star-Lore: An Illustrated Guide to the Star-lore and Constellations of Ancient Babylonia. Solaria Publications.

"Yellow Dragon," Wikimedia Foundation, last modified 13 August 2022, https://en.wikipedia.org/wiki/Yellow_Dragon

"Yellow Emperor," Wikimedia Foundation, last modified 29 July 2023, https://en.wikipedia.org/wiki/Yellow_Emperor

ABOUT THE CAELI INSTITUTE

A library with a presence on real land

CAELI SITS ON THE ORIGINAL HOMELANDS of the Coast Salish people, at the instersection of the Nisqually and Cowlitz Tribes, within the area specified by the Treaty of Medicine Creek (1854). When land wasn't ceded through good faith efforts, it was often stolen from our Indigenous relatives. *She-nah-nam* has been home to these people for thousands of years and we honor and respect their continued presence. It is important to understand the longstanding history that has brought us all to reside on this land and to seek to understand our place within that history, even as we make it our work to understand the future.

The Celestial Arts Education Library is a member-supported research institute like no other. Our collection centers astrology in its myriad forms and the expression of celestial arts from all human cultures throughout history. We aim to right the wrongs perpetrated by scientific positivism and colonial capitalism's abuse of our craft.

Inside our walls you can research materials and artifacts found together in this way nowhere else. We are a collection of collections, and we preserve the tomes written by our ancestors, so you can build upon their works and push our field even further.

Beyond our walls, CAELi is a vibrant community united by our shared passion for cosmological inquiry. Whether you are fascinated by ancient astronomy, modern astro magic, or envisioning a celestial art of the future, CAELi is your homebase. Your HQ.

We encourage and foster deep exploration and discussion of cosmological topics, through research into the primary and secondary sources found in our physical library, as well as experimental classes in our virtual campus. We support publication of your work in various venues, such as books, magazines, or journals, such as this one!

Join CAELi today and join the fight to restore astrology's rightful place in the pantheon of legitimized knowledges. At CAELi you can push the boundaries of the celestial arts, elevate your insights to new heights, and contribute to a broader understanding of the rich field we call astrology. Are you in?

www.caeli.institute

www.ingramcontent.com/pod-product-compliance
Lightning Source LLC
Chambersburg PA
CBHW040252090526
44586CB00041B/2812